HEINEMANN G(
BEGINNE

GW01080164

ELIZABET

Anna and the Fighter

HEINEMANN

BEGINNER LEVEL

Series Editor: John Milne

The Heinemann Guided Readers provide a choice of enjoyable reading material for learners of English. The series is published at five levels – Starter, Beginner, Elementary, Intermediate and Upper. At **Beginner Level**, the control of content and language has the following main features:

Information Control

The stories are written in a fluent and pleasing style with straightforward plots and a restricted number of main characters. The cultural background is made explicit through both words and illustrations. Information which is vital to the story is clearly presented and repeated where necessary.

Structure Control

Special care is taken with sentence length. Most sentences contain only one clause, though compound sentences are used occasionally with the clauses joined by the conjunctions 'and', 'but', and 'or'. The use of these compound sentences gives the text balance and rhythm. The use of Past Simple and Past Continuous Tenses is permitted since these are the basic tenses used in narration and students must become familiar with these as they continue to extend and develop their reading ability.

Vocabulary Control

At **Beginner Level** there is a controlled vocabulary of approximately 600 basic words, so that students with a basic knowledge of English will be able to read with understanding and enjoyment. Help is also given in the form of vivid illustrations which are closely related to the text.

For further information on the full selection of Readers at all five levels in the series, please refer to the Heinemann Readers catalogue.

Anna did not sleep all night. She was excited. Early in the morning, her father called her.

'Come on, Anna! It's time to get up. It's a long way to the station.'

Anna got dressed and she was soon ready. She did not eat any breakfast. She was nervous. She was going to visit her aunt in Naira. She was going alone in a train for the first time.

Anna and her father left the village and began to walk to the station. It was a long way. They reached the station at midday.

Soon the train came. It was nearly empty. Anna got in. She was frightened. It was her first journey away from home.

'Your aunt will meet you at Naira,' her father said. 'Be careful now, Anna. Don't talk to any strangers.'

The train started suddenly. Soon it was going fast. Anna watched her father. He looked smaller and smaller; then he disappeared.

The train journey was very long. Anna looked out of the window. The fields, trees, villages and animals rushed past. After a long time, she began to feel sleepy. She was very tired. Slowly, she fell asleep.

Later, Anna woke up. It was dark outside. She felt small and lost. She was a long way from her village and her father.

There was a man in the carriage with her now. He had an ugly face, and he was very big and strong. His hair was very short. He looked bad and dangerous.

The man smiled at Anna.

'Hello,' he said. 'You're awake now, are you? Where are you going?'

Anna remembered her father's words. She did not say anything.

'Are you going to Polona?' asked the man.

Anna was surprised. 'No, to Naira,' she said.

'Naira!' said the man. 'But we passed Naira two hours ago! You were asleep.'

Anna wanted to cry. She sat very still. It was warm in the carriage, but Anna felt cold.

'We've passed Naira?' she asked.

'Yes,' said the man.

Anna thought of the journey back to Naira. How much did it cost? She did not have any money. She thought of her aunt at Naira Station.

'Don't worry,' said the man. 'I'll help you. What's your name?'

'Anna,' she said.

'My name is Sam,' said the man. 'You can trust me, Anna.'

Anna looked at Sam again. He was very ugly. He had a long scar on his face and he looked dangerous. But he seemed kind. Was he good or bad? Anna did not know.

The train began to slow down. Sam got up and looked out of the window. Anna saw a newspaper on Sam's seat. There was a photograph on the back page. It was Sam's photograph! Above the photograph was a headline: *This man is a dangerous fighter!*

Now Anna was sure. Sam was a bad man, and dangerous too. He was a criminal. Anna must be careful. She must get away from him quickly.

Sam left the window. 'We're coming into Polona now,' he said. 'Stay with me. I'll help you.'

The train stopped. Anna jumped up and ran to the door. She wanted to run away. The door was very heavy. She could not open it. Sam was standing behind her.

'I'll open it,' he said.

THIS MAN IS A DANGEROUS FIGHTER!

Anna wanted to run away, but she was frightened of Sam. She was tired and lost. Polona was a big town. Anna did not know anybody there. Sam called a taxi.

'Get in, Anna,' he said. Anna got in.

'The Boxer Hotel,' Sam said to the driver.

The taxi went a long way. The streets of Polona were wide and busy. There were lots of cars, and shops, and people.

The taxi turned into a small, dark street and stopped. Sam got out and paid the taxi driver. Anna looked up and down the street.

'Come on, Anna,' said Sam.

Anna could not run away. She was weak and slow. Sam was big and strong. She followed Sam into the hotel.

There was a café inside the hotel. It did not look very clean. Two men were drinking and playing cards. They saw Sam. One of them said, 'Hello, Sam! Come and have a drink. Who's the pretty girl?'

Sam took off his coat and sat down.

'Hello Tino, hello Bubs,' he said. 'This is Anna. She's lost.'

The men looked at Anna, and laughed. 'Lost, is she?' said Tino. 'Poor Anna. You're a lucky man, Sam. Have a drink!'

Sam gave Anna a chair. She sat down. She looked at the men. Tino had a moustache. Bubs did not have any front teeth. They looked tough.

The men were drinking. Tino gave Anna a glass.

'Come on, Anna,' he said. 'Drink some wine.'

Anna pushed the glass away. She thought, I mustn't eat or drink anything. These men will give me a drug. Then I will fall asleep.

Sam called the waiter. 'Bring some dinner,' he said. 'Bring some good, hot food.'

The waiter came with the food. Bubs put some of the food on a plate and gave it to Anna. It looked good and smelt delicious. Anna forgot about drugs and began to eat. She ate quickly and finished everything. She put her spoon down. The men were looking at her. They laughed. Anna was very frightened again.

'Come on, Anna,' said Sam. 'You're tired. You must go to bed now.'

He took her arm.

'Lock her door, Sam,' said Tino. 'There are bad men in Polona. You must keep her safe.'

Bubs laughed. 'Goodnight, Anna,' he said.

Sam took Anna upstairs and into a bedroom. Her heart was beating fast.

'Goodnight, Anna,' said Sam. He smiled at her. 'Don't worry. You are safe here.'

Anna did not say anything. Sam seemed kind. But she remembered the newspaper. Sam was dangerous and his friends looked dangerous too. She must escape.

Sam went out of the room and shut the door. He locked it and went downstairs. Anna sat on the bed and cried.

Downstairs, the men drank and played cards. Anna heard their voices. They were laughing. After a long time, she fell asleep.

Anna woke late. The sun was shining. She looked out of the window. The waiter was sitting outside in the street. He was smoking a cigarette and reading a newspaper.

Anna looked round the room. It was dirty. There was some old paper on the floor. In one corner, there was a small table with some things on it.

Anna had an idea. There was a biro on the table. She took the biro and picked up a piece of paper from the floor. She wrote:

PLEASE HELP ME
I want to go to Naira.
My aunt is waiting for me there.
I must escape from here. I have
no money and no friends.
Anna

She threw the note out of the window. The waiter picked it up. He read the note. He looked up and saw her. He smiled at her and went into the hotel.

———

Anna heard voices outside her room. Somebody unlocked the door. The waiter came in. There was somebody on the stairs behind him.

It's a policeman! thought Anna. He's brought a policeman.

She ran forward. It was Sam. He was holding her note in his hand.

'Good afternoon, Anna,' said Sam. 'You've slept very late. You must be hungry. Come and have some food. We're going soon.'

The waiter smiled at Sam. Anna understood. The waiter did not want to help her. He and Sam were friends.

Anna went downstairs with Sam and the waiter. They gave her some food, but she was not hungry. She did not eat or drink anything.

Sam went outside into the street. Anna heard voices. Sam was talking to a man. What were they planning? Sam came inside again.

'Come on, Anna, we must go now,' he said.

A taxi was waiting outside. Anna and Sam got in.

'Where are we going?' Anna asked.

Sam looked at her. 'I'll take you to your aunt later,' he said. 'First, I have an important job to do.'

Sam smiled. The smile twisted his face. He looked very ugly.

Soon the taxi stopped. Sam and Anna got out. They were outside a big building. There was a notice outside the building.

TULIP PROMOTIONS
PRESENTS

TODAY AT 3 o'clock

SAM
THE
FIGHTER
V
DANNY
THE TIGER
IN
THE
MUNICIPAL HALL
TODAY AT 3 o'clock
SATURDAY

Anna understood now. Sam was a boxer. 'Dangerous fighter' meant 'good boxer'. Sam was not a criminal.

Anna followed Sam into the building. It was a very big hall. There were seats on all sides. In the middle was the boxing ring.

Tino and Bubs were waiting for them.

'Stay here, Anna,' said Sam. 'Tino and Bubs will look after you. I must go now.'

Tino and Bubs shook Sam's hand. 'Good luck, Sam,' said Bubs.

'You'll win all right,' said Tino.

Anna smiled at Sam for the first time. 'Good luck, Sam,' she said.

Tino and Bubs took Anna to a seat beside the ring. Tino sat on one side of her and Bubs on the other. Anna sat quietly and waited. The two men talked excitedly.

'Sam's going to win,' said Tino.

'Of course he'll win,' said Bubs. 'He's the best fighter in the country.'

Anna listened. Sam was famous!

'Everybody wants him to win,' said Tino. 'Everybody likes him.'

'That's right,' said Bubs. 'Sam's a great boxer, and he's a good man, too.'

'I know a story about Sam,' said Tino. 'One night he was asleep in bed. He heard shouts in the street and he looked outside. A house was on fire. He ran outside. There was a child in the burning house. He went inside and saved the child. But he was badly hurt. His face was burned and he got a bad scar.'

'Poor Sam,' said Bubs. 'That's why he's so ugly!' They both laughed.

Anna was listening quietly. She now understood everything. She was safe with Sam. She felt sorry for him.

'Is the fight going to start soon?' she asked Tino.

'Yes, of course,' said Tino. 'It will start very soon.'

The hall was full of people now. Boys were selling cigarettes and sweets. Everybody was laughing and joking.

The referee was waiting in the ring. The audience was excited now.

'Sam! Sam! We want Sam!' they shouted.

Sam climbed into the ring. He was wearing short trousers and big boxing gloves. He raised both hands in the air.

The crowd was clapping. 'Sam! Sam! Sam!' they shouted.

The other fighter climbed into the ring. He was very big and strong.

'Here comes Danny,' said Tino. 'He's a very good fighter.'

Anna was worried.

'Don't you worry, Anna,' said Bubs. 'Sam's the best fighter in the country.'

The referee called the two boxers to the centre of the ring. He spoke to them quietly for a few moments. Then Sam and Danny shook hands. The two fighters went back to their corners and waited.

A bell rang and the fight began.

Danny was younger than Sam, but he was a good fighter. He moved fast. He tried to hit Sam, but Sam jumped away every time. Sam's arms were long. He moved very quickly. He hit Danny hard, many times.

Anna was very excited. Her hands held the seat tightly.

It was a long fight. Sam moved quickly. He hit Danny often, but Danny did not fall down.

Sam was getting tired. He was moving more slowly. Anna was worried. The crowd was shouting, 'Sam! Sam!'

Anna shouted, 'Sam! Sam! Come on Sam! Watch out!' Tino and Bubs were shouting too.

Danny hit Sam's face hard. Blood came out of Sam's nose and one of his eyes was nearly closed. But Sam did not stop. He ran forward and hit Danny with all his strength.

Danny fell over and lay still. The referee started to count.

'One . . . Two . . . Three . . . Four . . .'

Danny did not move.

'Five . . . Six . . . Seven . . .'

Danny tried to get up. He could not.

'Eight . . . Nine . . . Ten.'

Danny lay still. The fight was over. Sam was the winner.

Anna was laughing and clapping. 'Well done, Sam! Well done, Sam,' she shouted.

Nobody heard her. Everybody was shouting, 'Sam! We want Sam! We want Sam!'

Tino and Bubs took Anna to the dressing-room. Sam was resting.

'Hello, Sam,' said Anna. 'You were great.'

Sam was surprised. 'Hello, Anna,' he said. 'You're different now. You didn't talk to me before.'

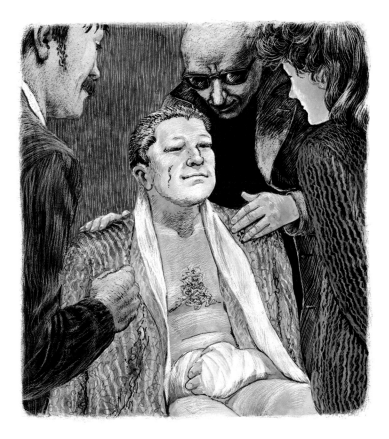

'I'm sorry, Sam,' said Anna. 'I was frightened . . .'

'I know,' said Sam. 'I'm big and ugly, and you were frightened. But I'm not a criminal, Anna.'

'I'm sorry, Sam,' Anna said again. 'I was wrong. I'm not frightened now.'

Sam was pleased.

'Come on, Anna,' he said. 'We'll go to Naira now. Your aunt is waiting for you.'

Anna said goodbye to Tino and Bubs. She got into a taxi with Sam. It was a long way to Naira and Anna asked Sam many questions. They talked, and talked, and talked. They reached Naira at night. It was dark.

Sam knew Naira. He quickly found Anna's aunt's house. They knocked on the door. The door opened.

Anna's aunt was standing in the doorway. She was crying.

'Oh Anna, Anna,' she said. 'Thank God! You are here at last.'

Then she saw Sam. He looked terrible. His face was cut and bruised after the fight.

'Anna!' she said. 'Who is this man?'

'Auntie,' Anna said. 'Don't be angry. This is Sam. I fell asleep on the train. I passed Naira Station. Sam helped me. He took me to a hotel. He brought me to Naira in a taxi.'

Anna's aunt looked at Sam again. 'Wait a minute,' she said.

She ran inside. She came back with a newspaper. Sam's photograph was on the back page.

'Are you Sam the boxer?' she asked.

'Yes, I am,' said Sam.

Anna's aunt was pleased. Sam was famous. He was a great man. Everybody knew him.

'Come in, Sam,' she said. 'Please sit down. Will you have some tea?'

Anna sat in the room with her aunt and Sam. She did not say anything. She felt very happy.

Anna's aunt asked Sam many questions. She laughed a lot. She liked him.

It was getting very late.

'I must go now, Anna,' said Sam. 'Can I come and see you again?'

'Yes, Sam,' said Anna.

She smiled at him.

Heinemann English Language Teaching
Halley Court, Jordan Hill, Oxford OX2 8EJ
A division of Reed Educational & Professional Publishing Limited

OXFORD MADRID FLORENCE ATHENS PRAGUE
SÃO PAULO MEXICO CITY CHICAGO PORTSMOUTH(NH)
TOKYO SINGAPORE KUALA LUMPUR MELBOURNE
AUCKLAND JOHANNESBURG IBADAN GABORONE

Heinemann is a registered trademark of Reed Educational & Professional
Publishing Limited

ISBN 0 435 27164 4

© Elizabeth Laird 1977, 1992
First published 1977
Reprinted nine times
This edition published 1992

A recorded version of this story is available on cassette.
ISBN 0 435 27274 8

Illustrated by Annabel Large
Typography by Adrian Hodgkins
Cover by Gill Sampson and Threefold Design
Typeset in 12/16 pt Goudy
by Joshua Associates Ltd, Oxford
Printed and bound in Malta by Interprint Limited

97 98 99 00 10 9 8 7 6